I CUT MY TONGUE ON A BROKEN COUNTRY

POEMS

KYO LEE

ARSENAL PULP PRESS
VANCOUVER

I CUT MY TONGUE ON A BROKEN COUNTRY

SECOND PRINTING: 2025

ARSENAL PULP PRESS
Suite 202 – 211 East Georgia St.
Vancouver, BC V6A 1Z6
Canada
arsenalpulp.com

The publisher gratefully acknowledges the support of the Canada Council for the Arts and the British Columbia Arts Council for its publishing program and the Government of Canada and the Government of British Columbia (through the Book Publishing Tax Credit Program) for its publishing activities.

Arsenal Pulp Press acknowledges the xʷməθkʷəy̓əm (Musqueam), Sḵwx̱wú7mesh (Squamish), and səlilwətaɬ (Tsleil-Waututh) Nations, custodians of the traditional, ancestral, and unceded territories where our office is located. We pay respect to their histories, traditions, and continuous living cultures and commit to accountability, respectful relations, and friendship.

Arsenal Pulp Press is committed to reducing the consumption of nonrenewable resources in the making of our books wherever possible. We make every effort to use materials that support a sustainable future. This book is printed on paper made with 100 percent sustainable recycled fibre content.

The following poems have been published, sometimes in different forms and under different titles: "lotus flower blooming into breasts" by CBC Books; "Why I Have Decided to Live" by *Narrative Magazine*; "Fish Market Wedding" and "Love Confession for My Mother" by *Nimrod International*; "The Rain, the Bamboo, the Burning" by *This Magazine*; "Manic Pixie Dreams" by *Under the Madness Magazine*; "Dreaming of Imaginary Wars" by *Touchstone Literary Magazine*; "out of the blue," "Mother Recites Her Will to Me," "Selective Misophonia," and "Yellow Noise" by the Writers' Trust of Canada.

Cover and text design by Jazmin Welch
Edited by Natalie Wee
Copy edited by Catharine Chen
Proofread by JC Cham

Printed and bound in Canada

Library and Archives Canada Cataloguing in Publication:
Title: I cut my tongue on a broken country : poems / Kyo Lee.
Names: Lee, Kyo, author.
Identifiers: Canadiana (print) 20240447751 | Canadiana (ebook) 2024044776X | ISBN 9781551529776 (softcover) | ISBN 9781551529783 (EPUB)
Subjects: LCGFT: Poetry.
Classification: LCC PS8623.E4424 I23 2025 | DDC C811/.6—dc23

ADVANCE PRAISE FOR *I CUT MY TONGUE ON A BROKEN COUNTRY*

"Exquisite details permeate this debut collection. We follow a narrator whose worlds and self are fractured and mending. We hear translations, gasps, and 'tongue on tender rabbit meat.' The narrator is both the lifeless rabbit and the killer, riding trains through dimensions of memory, time, and place."
—LEANNE DUNIC, AUTHOR OF *WET* AND *ONE AND HALF OF YOU*

"Formally inventive, playful, and tender, these poems are resoundingly alive. Not since Susan Musgrave has such a young poet burst onto the scene fully formed, writing heartbreakingly perfect poetry. Kyo Lee will continue to astound you with her wisdom, depth of talent, and unflinching eye."
—SARAH TSIANG, AUTHOR OF *GRAPPLING HOOK*

"*i cut my tongue* weaves heartbreak, sex, malice, temptation, devastation, and defiance into a powerful coming-of-age collection. Deftly moving through languages, landscapes, and time, Kyo Lee builds us a lattice to scale as we navigate Orientalism, familial expectation, loss of religion, and emerging queer identity to carve out new lexicons and a redefined sense of love."
—ELLEN CHANG-RICHARDSON, AUTHOR OF *BLOOD BELIES*

"*i cut my tongue* teems with contrast: rebellious energies of electric flights crash into questions about forgiveness and repair. Kyo Lee presents readers with a bewitchingly noir portrait—burning with imagery of drowned cities, archetypal families, lovers, teeth, rabbits, snakes, Korean mosquitos, and holy water. Lee's romantic, hungering speakers are often surprised by their own liminality: 'i forgot the weight of my own spine in the water,' as memories interrupt with the force of their own pulsing agendas."
—SUN YUNG SHIN, AUTHOR OF *THE WET HEX* AND *UNBEARABLE SPLENDOR*

MORE PRAISE FOR *I CUT MY TONGUE ON A BROKEN COUNTRY*

"Absolutely incandescent. Every stanza is a revelation, every line a reverberation. In Kyo Lee's hands, language becomes both a banner and blaze. An astounding debut from an arresting new voice, shot through with rare and dazzling light. I wish I could have grown up with this book, and I am so glad to live in a world where it exists."

—GINA CHUNG, AUTHOR OF *SEA CHANGE* AND *GREEN FROG*

To myself

CONTENTS

효 / 孝 / hyo

한 / 恨 / han

청 / 靑 / chung

정 / 情 / jung

효
孝
hyo

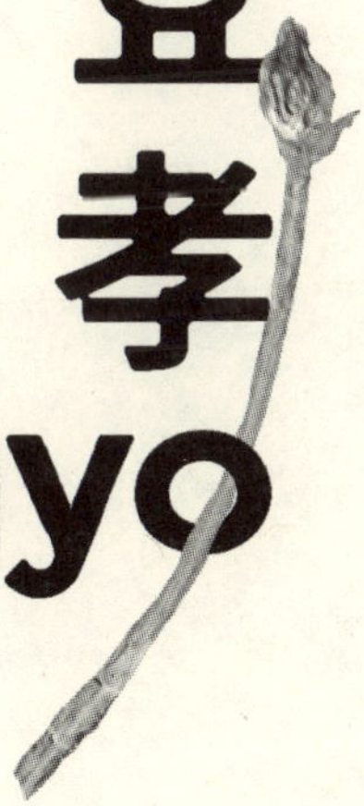

Great & Green

You come home to your mother
at the cutting board slicing money
into green cards.

She says *We're moving*. In the car
she practises the word *permanent* as if
it might make home inside her.

Says it until it no longer
feels real. *Where are we going again?*
Time is moving away from us.

Tomorrow we will run faster
stretch out our arms
into bluer skies. Was it this city

where your mother comes home at 2 a.m.
leftover apples in hand?
You were starving

& she forgot why & you tucked away
belonging into the back pocket of your jeans.
Air smells different in each city.

Here, like money & stevia.
It was in the city of rainy corn & ghostly hearts
you learned to stop recognizing faces

at parties. Started only attending ones
                    you wouldn't mind leaving.
          You learned how to decorate

yourself with desperation.
          Rouged your lips with spices & apology.
A boy asked if you were illegal

& you didn't know. You were eleven
          & thought about marrying him
said *i do* enough times to forget

                    what you agreed to.
Every year life expires
& renews in freshly breathing cities

          where window lights glow deep into the night.
We flutter like moths
          to their moonlike glow. Wings

split on the window but we beat on,
          boats against the current
borne back ceaselessly into the past.

can you be a poet & be happy?

The sky has been pregnant with rain for weeks now.
I wait for monsoon season, the sky's swinging underbelly
thumping with the heartbeats of an unborn child.
I don't look at sunsets the way I used to.
I love out of duty.
Van Gogh did not eat yellow paint to get happiness inside him.
He ate it to kill himself.
I want to smear paint all over myself
& then fall from the sky. Colourful monsoon.
Art is not because of but in spite of pain.
I want to believe this.
But yesterday I started writing poetry again
& stockpiled single-use razors under my bed.
Every poem has a beating heart.
To find it, burn it holy. My edges are on flames.
Why has no one ever asked can you be a poet & be sad?
On the bike ride home my thighs purple
like rotten autumn plums on the plastic seat.
At her house when her grandmother slapped my face
I was already thinking of metaphors.
I said goodbye too quickly
bought ice tea & a razor on the way home.
The only material you have is pain. Now paint.
If I ever ask for help
tell me to finish what I've started.

Fish Market Wedding

sometimes i think about marrying a woman just to piss off my mother / i'll wear a scarlet leather dress & let vengeance trail my back like a veil / dance down the fish market / ice blocks & raw dead things clapping for us from either side / when the oyster merchant / pronounces us / woman & woman / i'll swim through her mouth / pierce pearls through her spine / the ceremony will take place in the crisp moments / between yesterday & today / when the world becomes soft / & fishermen drown their boats / & merchants bathe in red tubs / golden nooses / of squid lights illuminate the aisle / as i walk down / stepping over dead fish with no eyes & gaping gills / hungry / for something they do not want / i recognize him / yes / from my plate / when mother used to cook mackerels / she picked out the eyeballs to put on my spoon / watched me swallow / as she sucked on the skeleton / *the greatest kind of love* / she said / *is sacrifice* / at my fish market wedding / i will wade into the sea / & catch a fish with my bare hands / & drop the squirming piece of life / into my mother's empty mouth

i hope death is not cold

My aunt said that if she could die
        she would fill a small room with lilies until
their scent filled the room floor to ceiling until

        the room became heaven. A Korean myth
that lilies smell so good that in your sleep
        you want to keep inhaling & forget to exhale.

To die for the insatiable desire for beauty.
        i reinvent myself into a clear vase
something you could fill with ocean

        or tea or girlhood or any other beautiful thing.
i would die for metaphorical resonance.
        i, too, have fantasized about lily rooms:

when would my heart give up? i reinvent myself
        into green this time. Things that live
for the sake of living. Funny thing is when she did die

        it wasn't even beautiful.
Not even lilies growing out of dilated pupils
        pollen sprinkled on an open stomach.

Not even capital *T* Tragedy.
        Sterile. Hospital walls widening to fit carcasses
whiter than death. i wondered if this was heaven.

How could you die
like this? Now i reinvent myself into thin cotton
bedsheets warping around other bodies.

i hope death is not a cold thing.
i've brought you lilies.

"What does your name mean?"

Kyo

Beauty (姣), moonlight (晈), laughter (噭), to teach (敎), to choke (絞). Unite (協) in Japanese. To draw a line down your name & watch the gap widen into parallel barricades. Apricot (杏) in Japanese. Your taemyeong was Apricot because you were so small & sour & spring. The things we end up meaning by accident. To go by Sarah in dressing rooms because you're tired. To answer to pauses. To say your own name like a bullet caught between the teeth.

Eun

Grace (恩), silver (銀), edge (垠), to growl (狺), to suffer (慇), to be green as grass (蒑). To sever pieces of your name like wishbone. To hang in the air like a collapsed promise. As if abandoning a name is all you need to become something new.

Lee

Hometown (里), wound (痍), foreign intruder (夷), a boy resting under an apricot tree (李). You want to sit down beside him, forget your name & pick a warm fruit to share. You dream of a world where your name is Apricot Apricot Apricot. A world where three wrongs make a right.

Sarah

Your pastor tries to baptize you with Dasani & calls you Sarah. You wonder if your god can pronounce your name.

____ ____ ____

Beautiful Suffering. Silver Choking. Moonlit End. Water Song Bird Song. Apricot Apricot. Whatever you want it to.

Nameless Prayers

If her eyes were windows they were stained
glass. The soul shimmered in a collage of light
as we snuck into the church

    our figures fading into the purple of nightfall.
    Praying that my mother missed me
    more than she loved God. What would God say

if Jesus came out to him?
She covered my eyes before kissing me
like God forbidding Lot to witness

    his burning city. Of course
    i looked because i wanted to be frozen
    in time. Melting at the sight of our destruction.

My guts were flooding
with all of her whispered heat.
The second time my city has drowned.

    Here are the unnamed people in the Bible:
    Noah's wife / Ham's wife / Nimrod's wife
    Lot's wife / Laban's wife / Potiphar's wife

Simeon's wife / Job's wife / the serpent.
i knelt for the first time in years
to warm myself to the heat of hell.

To try to find my name, burning.
i imagined my mother on her knees
worshipping virgins & flesh & names.

i wished that we were all Jesus
enough to love before forgiving.
But i was never daughter

enough to let myself be sacrificed.
Did Jesus also pick at his scabs
& hum in the shower & stargaze?

This human thing is not a phase, God!
You wouldn't get it. He also wouldn't get
how i baptized myself on the serrated edges

of stained glass & rainwater.
It was all burning down. The city.
The church. The names. She asks

Do you think hell has flowers?
I redefine love from sin
to saviour.

I laugh wide enough to fit Jerusalem
through my open mouth.
I open my eyes.

Your City

in memory of the Gwangju Uprising

It's the girl with the bowl cut & red bandana
        chasing hope in the truck's exhaust fumes losing
herself around the corner. It's my aunt

young & running into the future.
        It's my aunt naked & roped on the military truck
body bled & bruised into a red & blue taegeuk.

Maybe it's her brother across the barricade
        beating breath out of bodies. Green boots
imprinting maps to afterlife onto necks. Not a brother

for now. For now, soldier. For now, Korea.
        For now, kill & then pray it wasn't your sister.
Is that a red bandana?

Lost between fragmented taxi cabs
        shattered glass & legs with no destination
cornering you into the city. No exit

out of this mess. *Your* mess. *Your* people. *Your* city
        built from *your* ashes.
Your city stripped bare like a winter tree

& clubbed into a past. It's my aunt
        fighting. Voice fractured. Skin splattered.
Is it my aunt

over there, one of the people buried in flags?
        History doesn't remember faces.

Warmly, Lucifer

[1] Do you remember when Father told me I was his most beautiful creation?

[2] Honestly, I didn't know it at the time [3] how I bore light [4] in every crevice of my flesh. [5] I was a damn pretty crier. [6] I wish I had known this so I could have properly wept like an angel.

[7] Of course, the fall hurt. If it looked like lightning, it hurt like a storm. [8] But every time I touched my shoulder blades [9] I didn't think of Father, I thought of you, Michael, pressed my scars trying to recall your face.

[10] I didn't know how frail humans are. In this body, living is a risk. I had to learn its fragility [11] before its beauty. [12] I am nowhere near as beautiful [13] as I once was but my lover reminds me every morning, when I am covered in white bedsheets, that I look angelic. [14] When he says this, his face becomes pink as dawn & he looks like you.

[15] Yesterday, we baked cherry pie from the fruit we picked together, [16] singing in a rainy August orchard & on the first bite, I decided [17] I don't want to return to heaven.

[18] You would not believe how magical humans are when observed closely. [19] They kiss each other on the forehead, [20] splash water just to sense the coldness. [21] All I have to do is sneeze & my lover blesses me with Father's name.

[22] I am no longer a pretty crier, Michael, but this lover, [23] he holds me like a child. [24] This man, he gives rain to plants every morning & returns smelling like roses & fog. [25] The way he touches me [26] as if touching a flower, a life not done growing, makes me like being [27] fragile. When I touch my shoulder blades [28] I think of him. [29] I've given up being holy to be whole.

[30] If you ever choose to visit, I will run to welcome you with these small human feet that hurt & trip [31] & we'll bake you cherry pie.

Love Is a Stranger Every Day

Loving you was an act of rebellion.
i stab my tongue through your throat in love

with the image of my father crying
until he understands what it means to break

softly. Love is a stranger every day.
Love can only be spoken in metaphors.

Does it matter why i loved you
if i did? Does it matter why i trembled in your arms?

It's always easier to clutch you tighter
than to let you go. i'm a hoarder

of people. i'm out of breath.
Do i have the patience for regret?

Do you have the patience to hold me tighter?
My father believes that i'm a good girl

who doesn't kiss other girls
who cut my lips stripper red

& leave my eyes bloodshot with hope.
My father believes that i'm a smart girl

who knows when to break away from a kiss
to breathe. Dear Heavenly Father,

go suck a dick. Or maybe i mean forgive me.
What do you ask of me when my body is sacrilege?

Maybe i only loved you to teach myself defiance.
Does it matter?

Learned Anatomy

My mother & I brainstorm all the places
I could get plastic surgery.
A weekly bonding activity:
we circle limbs & gossip & eat
Costco yakgwa to fill all the calories
my imaginary self is missing out on.
Raise the nose bridge a little.
There's a new hanyak good for weight loss.
Botched attempt at love.
We share one roll of double-eyelid tape
& talk about everything unimportant.
We look nothing alike except
for a lump in the throat from trying not to say *I love you.*
I do, of course, but
we don't have to talk about it.

Turing Test to Differentiate Poet & AI

How do you love?

I bury my heart like a punishment.
Once I found a girl
at the bottom of a pool. I scooped her up
& put her under my tongue like a coin.
She unzipped me & everything fell:
bloody machinery, maps to Silicon Valley,
the void. Caressing the void, wet hair on limbs
I thought for the first time
it may not be a burden to live.

Where do you come from?

A world of burning. From Eve.
From the apple. We are composed of sin.
My country was crashing down. I stood
witnessing its last bits burning in the red wind.
We all have our own mechanical wombs.

What happened that August night you returned
with ashes & the moon?

To be a proper daughter is to kill.
I am full of shuddering & visions
that cannot be turned off with sleep.
I was startled at the hollowness
of my walking. I put my head on her chest
& it thundered as if fighting nature
to stay alive.
Aren't we all trying to be human?

Describe a sunset.

The world is bleeding.
To be human is to forgive most beautiful things.
Orange clouds, purple murmurs.
Is anything above the ground the sky?
Say yes.
Say we are flying.

What have we lost in the artifice of being?

Everything.

Selective Misophonia

/ nails on the chalkboard / nails on skin / metal chopsticks scraping the bottom of metal ramen pots / korean mosquitos / quiet provinces / the word *gyopo* / how i can't stop fucking saying *libary* despite knowing i'm wrong / english speakers saying *oppa* / the moon inflating during autumn / the piling loudness of yesterdays / my mother sighing / my mother saying *gay* / poet voices / scissors cutting things not intended to be cut / American mosquitos / slurping guk / *gook* / silence /

Yellow Noise

My father can't sleep through silence.
He says silence is too loud

so he drowns himself in YouTube videos
about North Korea's dictatorships,

gentrification, Britain's colonies,
things that only vaguely remind him of home.

He sleeps on the floor. That reminds him
of being home or poor or something.

The bed is too silent & too white & too his
& too comfortable, causes too much sleep.

Maybe he wants to stop dreaming
about expired dreams. Ghost-white, ghost-silent

ghost dreams about white beds & orange juice
& money. Maybe he's becoming America

& its relentless noise. The best way
to survive in this country's cacophony

is to shut the fuck up. We know this.
He wakes up every three hours

gasping for noise & i pretend
not to hear him.

한
恨
han

One day the ordinaries will change

& I will attempt to recall half memories of a spring afternoon, one of the thousands of days that are too ordinary to feel the need to remember.

We're lying under a willow tree or a maple tree or just a tree—all I know is that I've been watching patches of light waltz on your face as you read a book. You roll to your side & show me a passage you like. I pretend to read it but I can't focus because you've highlighted almost every word on the page & scribbled plants in the margins. I want to hold your hand and squeeze it but instead I tell you that you're defying the purpose of highlighting & at this point I can only see the blank parts of the page. You say that sometimes you need to notice the ordinary.

It's a warm night on the same day or maybe a different day, it's hard to tell, really, because it hasn't been highlighted. The sky is littered with stars but actually I'm not sure because I never wear my glasses & to be honest, I can barely see the moon when you tell me that full moons are your favourite surprises. I tell you that they're not surprises at all but you tell me that we only notice them when we want to.

I hope I also said things you will write poems about though anything I can say seems ordinary. How was I supposed to know that one day I would give anything to watch you read & to love a blurry moon?

how to become a god of summer evenings

The kind of nights where moonlight is damp on the skin:
that's how i remember every night of that summer.
Why do i suffer nostalgia
for memories i don't want to remember?
Weird how we kept our rat poison
in a pretty green jar
in our medicine cabinet. Weird
how pain is lineal.

Do you remember when we were younger
the cat brought a rabbit half alive & half open
so we poked at its heart with a stick?
i want it to be that summer again
stealing fireballs & glances at each other.
We buried the rabbit
& then our hands. Young
under the undressing sky.
Maybe i should be grateful for the things i can't remember:
there must be a reason why
i only remember your soft feet that night
& not what stained them
or the red shower
or where we buried that rabbit.

On nights when moonlight was damp on the skin
i threatened god
that i'd better be dead by next morning.

But god does not grant freedom
to cowards afraid to get blood on their own hands.
My scars are almost gone now
paper thin & beautiful.
What if no evidence of my past exists?

You step out of the coin karaoke

into the Dongdaemun streets where throbbing
lights & technicolour dreams flood the sidewalks
sweep you up in their current.

Everything temporary & edible:
tanghulu strawberries, neon signs, karaoke
bar girls in rhinestone dresses

tugging at your wrists to stay.
You're getting tipsy on the noise
& the pull of what you can't have

anymore. All the bright things:
street lights, headlights, cigarettes,
people's eyes—they could make a small sun

of their own. Think about the strangers
bustling around you, guess
their favourite fruits & phobias.

Feel the chill of the violet glow
from the thousand open signs swimming
on your skin, how it makes you feel sexy.

You're thinking that youth is green in colour.
The city has been saturated
since the last time you walked here

with your mother, eating tornado potatoes
& not thinking about anything at all
& smiling & smiling & smiling.

You're thinking about your mother.
You imagine her a year younger than you are
walking in front of you in a denim skirt

& breezy steps. On her way to a tteokbokki place
she's thinking that the moon is bright tonight
almost like an artificial sun.

She's thinking of her dead father.
She's thinking about the boy who looks damn good
in Calvin Klein jeans. (He is not your father.)

She's trying not to think about her mother
squatting in the moonless alley the next street over
tainted with that cold violet glow & soiled money.

She's thinking that youth is the colour green.
She's not thinking about you.
She's not thinking about how she'll comb your hair

while telling you stories
about the Dongdaemun streets. She's not thinking
about buying the watermelon

you said you were craving yesterday.
She's not thinking about you climbing out
of the window to get lost in the neon night.

No, she's not thinking about you at all
when she giggles with her friends about the love note
she left in that boy's gym shoes

& steps into the coin karaoke.

The Rain, the Bamboo, the Burning

It's raining. Bamboo skeletons rattling the night.
        i'm wearing my old red jacket
actually, *your* old red jacket
        though only i ever wear it.
How can things belong
        to me without ever being mine?
How can i be jealous when my language
        sounds sweeter in your mouth?
Let's sneak into the temple.
        i kiss your lips briefly.
We fit each other like sanded puzzles.
        i let you go.
Let you dance between the bamboo.
        Let you pull me into the scent
of burning inside the temple.
        Time has stopped for us.
For this beloved nonbelonging.
        You whistle into me
until the forest
        pulsates with our breaths.
i don't love you anymore.
        Not like this.
Not like i could belong to you
        without ever being yours.
But i love you & i will love you
        & i will love the rain
& the bamboo
        & the burning.

Moon Town

우리는 살고 싶다

The street lights are so orange, the alleyway looks like it's burning. Under flimsy blue roofs, middle-aged women grab at every stumbling man's wrists, measuring beats of wildness. The night is so blue, faces resemble bruises. The girls inside the whimpering houses slip back into white dresses to preserve the shame of being stripped. Across the river, a boy & I pedal a swan boat silently. Seat damp with sweat, I pedal intensely to make it back in the rental time limit, thinking of everything but the boy, thinking of the ripples, how we disturb everything in our path. We paid for this. We paid to end where we started & gain nothing in the middle. The alleyways have been called Miari Texas ever since the War's aftermath of military prostitution—thank you American soldiers for saving our economy, we'll name our red-light districts after your spaghetti westerns. Only a few fistfuls of dollars here, wrinkled inside panties, a girl worth as much as a swan boat rental. A week ago, I met a different boy in the burning alleyway. He put out his cigarette on the tender part of my neck where I wanted to be kissed, pulled me into the streets where scents of cheap alcohol & piss bloomed from the ground. Before Miari Texas, the city was called Moon Town because, after the government demolished the war refugees' makeshift houses, residents could see the moon from their homes. On the river, the moon paints mirages of itself, beautiful lies surrounding us. We cut through the reflections, angry. Before the swan boats, we went to a Korean BBQ named Moon Town where we paid the price of two girls to witness the redness of meat before we devoured it. Before all this, Miari was one big grave for people killed during the Japanese colonization of Korea. This life is too wild to be translated. One has to wonder *how did we get here* especially when one needs to ride a swan boat back to shore & one's legs have started to cramp. Before I was born, the girls used to dance behind glass doors like displays, adorned with pink light & stares, a mirage. Every night there is sex on top of mounds of corpses. The grave only gets bigger. I have tried arranging & rearranging every yesterday but at every instance I end up here, against the Moon Town boy, scraping my back on the graffitied brick wall. I lose myself in the corner of his boyish smirk, pain-stained mouth. It feels like every tragedy has compounded to this moment but isn't this true for every moment? I vow to stop making this about myself, but I break my promise again, on my knees, praying to his leather shoes. I am one of the moon's mirages, restless as the dead. Soon, this town will be gentrified & so will I. Dear swan boy, are you home safely? Dear girls in white dresses, are you home?

Field Notes from Time

The train back from Seoul.
        The world outside is turning green
& time is slowing down. The sun is lower here

& we run west to beat it to its end.
        Crumbled mountains, gutted tunnels
& old ladies crouched on the floor

selling small ugly purses. Is this home?
        i've defined home by its lack of definition.
Shrugged. There is no word for home in Korean.

i have lived all my summers
        on this train, pretending i have somewhere to go
& nostalgic for the future. i sucked the metal

edges of empty pop cans to scythe my lips
        on sweetness. Pressed my nose to the window
& tried to see the wind. i've yearned

for a time to return to
        as if at a train station waiting for life to begin.
i think about my father, the one i left

alone
        with one carton of eggs in the apartment.
Inside the train is a world

constantly on the move.
        Motion sickness for time.
There is an incessant shaking in here

a rumbling of the heart as we forget
        our stops. i start writing a letter
to my father now, while i still love him,

& postmark it for three months later.
        Love is a practised thing.
i think about equal & opposite reactions.

        Is my father somewhere
back in his apartment erasing my letters?
        i've forgotten where i am going.

There is no place to return.

I hope the world ends

with both a bang & a whimper.
We were a worthwhile disaster.
Spring is eerie this year
overly sweet lavenders
& the scent of warm roadkill.

The best part of a jigsaw puzzle
is the breaking.
To destroy everything
we've worked for
with our own disgusting hands.

Every start is the start of an end.
Doom runs silently under our skin.
We inherited this
from God. God, don't let us fall apart
with time.
Gradual endings are hard to grieve.

I want us to be a fire
that has to be extinguished.
I want to be shambles, fists of dust, skeletons
fitting like wrong pairs of jigsaw.

The sky bares its teeth.
We prepare for doomsday
with sundresses & clementines.
We have made something out of nothing.
Nothing out of something?

Indie rock songs in the background
crescendo preparing for the closing credits.
The world has ended
many times before us.
One day
I will regret this wish to know suffering.

on messy teenage martyrdom

She tells me that one day, i'll miss her.
She tells me to shut up so quietly
that i have to listen. Hunched
against the bathroom wall she says puking
is a practice of art, an act of self-discipline,
the only time we get to retrieve a past
mistake. i swallow more of her than i can keep
salvaging history on the bathroom floor.
She devours me so carefully
as if to thread the bones out of a living fish:
i fall through her fingers like rain. Late summer
dyes my wrists crimson but she kisses it off.
What we call love: counting the calories
in each other's shot glasses, eleven-dollar vodka
& bleeding gums.
i open the window
until the night leaks into the room & moonlight
slips through our lips. She kills
her cigarette on her palms, fire
nailing holes.
Jesus, let me hold you.
This is how we become yesterday.
She pulled me closer.
Until i could feel my breath
dissolving in her Sacred Heartbeats.
It's night. It's always night.
Her limp limbs flooding into mine, still warm.

i think of her
goneness a crucifixion for our sins.
She told me *One day you're going to miss me*
& i laughed & said *Then don't leave.*
1 Peter 4:8 *Above all, keep loving one another earnestly,*
since love covers a multitude of sins.

Last Words as Vows

모든 죽어 가는 것을 사랑해야지—윤동주, 서시

– "I live." —Caligula

Someone has died since your last breath. But you knew this. There is neither novelty nor nobility in death. You be the one to tell death this horrendous truth. You are closer to her.

– "A party! Let's have a party." —Margaret Sanger

In Korean, the words for grave
& oxygen are the same.

산소 (san-so): what makes the mountains

When I say san-so
it tastes fresh like a summer
in which no one dies.

To love a dying thing.
To say I love loving you
more than I love being
okay.

산소 (san-so): what we need to stay alive

– “Et tu, Brute?” —Julius Caesar

For every inhale, you breathe one atom
from Julius Caesar’s last breath.

People and senators, be not affrighted

But were *you* affrighted, Brutus?
Him sticking to your chest

blood to blood
did you answer him under your breath

And you, Caesar?
How come you are dying?

– “Now comes the mystery.” —Henry Ward Beecher

Even as I was
        planning to kill myself
I only thought of death
        as the absence of living.
Intangible as burning
        your hand on a star.

I hope death is more
        than I can imagine.
I hope death is a campfire
        spreading to the forest.
I hope death is a blanket
        softer than a secret.
I hope death opens its arms to you
        like the morning glory
to the sun.

– "Don't you dare ask God to help me." —Joan Crawford

Grief is a house
we build on the edge of darkness.

I stand in the kitchen
witness the darkness darken

through the windows as I do the dishes.
I break every dish knowing

I am the only one who can
pick up the pieces of my violence.

Mirrored Self-Portrait as Frog & Man

am i the red stain on the rock
or the frog that it crushed?

i was still tender when my father
flung a frog to the rock

the scent of death
travels slowly

during the war my grandfather
swallowed frogs whole & living

throat widening
into the gates of an empty hell

eyes dripping with grisly voracity
to harbour two heartbeats in one body

how powerful it feels
to hold breath in one palm

& violence in the other
how do i abandon this want for violence

war parasites off a country's hunger
dear father, dear boy with a croaking voice

begging at American feet for a life
dear starlight, dear swaying rice

wash the red stains away
the boundary between a kiss & a bite is teeth

the boundary between saviour & surrender
is as thin as my father

snakes must swallow their food whole
because they have the wrong teeth

my father no longer has teeth, instead
manhood clobbered into his gums

what ugly rituals does it take
to lure hunger into the body

what ugly rituals does it take
to lure hunger out of the body

& how do i perform?

Dreaming of Imaginary Wars

A dream in which you're falling forever
into the arms of a bleeding sunrise
spilling sea water from its bullet holes.
i dress its wounds with my lips. It's a dream in which

i swaddle my father in cotton blankets & sing
him to sleep. i've inherited his gunpowder bones.
He's inherited my ceramic girlhood. i kiss his forehead.
i steal his dagger to cut up the sun

staggering into dusk. Time has escaped us.
The past disappears inches behind my feet.
The sun undresses into a starry skeleton
& i'm reminded of his rib cage, traceable over skin.

i lost pieces of myself everywhere.
In the crib, in the splinters, in my father …
i'm trying to scavenge myself in lost parts of the world.
What will be left when everything is over?

Who will wake me up?

Lotus Blossom Drowning

"How would you like to go to America, Lotus Flower?" (The Toll of the Sea)

i wake up / as love interest crawling / out of a lotus flower / pearl-white torso / sticky with tadpole guts & divinity / baby face / & legs split open / like countries

"I proud to be good girl." (The World of Suzie Wong)

i wake up to my mother / beheading / a lotus flower from its root / with a butcher's knife / *Men will fall in love / once / you feed them this*

"I will love you if that is your desire." (Sayonara)

i cradle the decapitated lotus flower to my chest / which is to say / i love too much / for beauty & not enough for sustenance / which is to say / i will fall in love with anything beautiful / : / beheaded flowers / the silver of bone after a gash / American boys

"One of these boys might be your ticket out." (Miss Saigon)

yes / i take America / to be my lawfully wedded GI husband

"Me so horny." (Full Metal Jacket)

i suck his dick / in the knife-red washroom stalls of a Korean BBQ /
oh America / can you find a country inside my stomach? / slice it down the
middle / & start carving / *oh America* / i dream of becoming / your liminal
space / let me sink / let me cook you lotus roots / let me feed you /
real hunger

청
青
chung

tradition of running toward tragedy

Pompeii / October 79 AD   Itaewon / October 2022

October is the season of death

the girls do not think of this
the girls dress up as time
head to the streets with baskets of dried fruit
celebrate preserving life beyond its limits
like jewels in the ashes fingers
clutching to every moment
sifting through dried plums & grapes & figs
the ground groans

danger is a thing of the past

how fast a city falls apart

when the sky erupts into plea
grounds shiver with footsteps
girls run home fists full of last breaths
as skeletons pile into mounds it is unfair
to die at the hands of our own people
to die of our own foolishness

the fire is catching up

Field Notes from Murder

Next to the graves i meet a snaggle-toothed boy.
        He reminds me of the rabbit i killed
sweet eyes with an innocence that kindles violence
        or is it envy? i ask if he believes
in an afterlife. He says *I'm still living.*

He confesses that he has never killed before.
        i give him my pocket knife & prayer.
i almost wanted him to be god.
        i ask if he has seen the dead man in Chinatown
crumpled under the peach stand, nectarines

littered around his corpse. *Maybe he was sleeping.*
        Maybe that's what we all said
as we picked up peaches, pressed into their skin
        & put all the bruised ones back.
i wish i hadn't killed the rabbit.

i rub the rabbit's foot in my pocket
        & vow to stop wearing grief on my sleeve.
Did you know cicadas live in a state of dormancy
        for years? Not dead but not living.
He nods. *Aren't their songs beautiful tonight?*

i could have been a better girl
        rabbit / lover / hunter / martyr / murderer.
He returns my pocket knife, keeps the blessing.
        i'm still living. i'm still living.
i remind myself of the rabbit i killed.

푸르다

Waiting for my flight, you hold my hand
        & we start the clapping game
with the song about the rabbit.

푸른 하늘 은하수

You went to Korea last summer
        to become beautiful.
Returned brokenly so, double eyelids

& sun-skinny. My turn.
        My favourite word is 푸름
because i cannot define it except

with a world so young & green
        the horizon moves away as you run
toward it. Because it's an adjective.

        Because how can something
so complete
        mean nothing when alone.

토끼 한 마리

The way the children sing it
        there are three rabbits:
one fried, one steamed, one escaping

to the west. i hate this part. i'm sorry.
    i've worn my green card like a raincoat.
i've warmed myself on fires

that killed. i abandoned shame
    three choruses ago
tongue on tender rabbit meat.

가기도 잘도 간다 서쪽 나라로

Lost count
    of the lives i've wasted
trying to be 푸름.

Let's start again.
    The flight is boarding.
Let's sing the rabbits home.

out of the blue

아닌 밤중에 홍두깨 (rolling pin in twilight) is a Korean proverb used to describe an inexplicable action. It originated from the Joseon dynasty when widowed women were required to remain celibate by a law punishable by death. Nevertheless, men would sneak into the widowed women's homes at night to rape them, causing the women to fear anyone finding out. "Rolling pin," a euphemism for male genitalia, refers to the unexpected disaster that found these widowed women during the night.

Strange how noises, too, have accents.
The rolling pin beats the light out of the night
& i can hear its strained teeth & uncomfortable
infusions of *R*'s and *L*'s,
soju stuck in the spaces between
teeth.
There are proverbs in Korean
with no English equivalent.
i break my tongue
to become a new one, one that isn't as meaty
& oppressive on America's lips.

i am rolled out thin & blue
under your blunt wooden hits until i blend
with the night sky.
My father's teeth are the colour of stars
fading away, with no one to miss them.
But i sometimes miss him.
On cold nights when the stars deflate
with a whisper, i find the sea

& think of him.
        i crawled out of the womb
feet first: an act of defiance.
Father named me "song of water & birds."
        It is not as beautiful in English.
        i am not as beautiful in English.

        There are some proverbs in Korean
that i wish to not remember in English.
        i reach into the sky & rub stardust into my wrists.
i jump off the moon
        & meet my father at the bottom of the ocean.
The nights when we collide
        like wet meat & rolling pin
        night sky & stars
He
        beats the skies
over & over & over again.

        i watch the life drip out of my father:
oil spilling out from a roadkill deer.
        Red stains my surface. i don't know
where it came from—
blood or womanhood
        or why not both.

How to Have a Hot Girl Summer

☑ *Die*

your hair blue. Stain the undersides of your nails
in the process. Remember how liquid colour clots
in your grasp, like bruises piling up in forgotten
places. Think about hanging yourself
then forget it. You don't want your dead weight
pulling down the sky.

☑ *Starve*

Imagine your blue hair as a nighttime pool
imitating naturalness in its destruction of the natural.
Imagine your frame a sickly shining skeleton sliced
into shimmerings of the moon on the pool surface. Even light
mistaking you for what you are not. Oh
isn't it beautiful?

☑ *Forget*

yourself in the time. Watch yourself outside the window
bicycling & faceless. You made this window
from your mirror & cut yourself on it in the process.
Do you see now
how the world is only an echo of yourself?

☑ *Take*

your shirt off. Lean against the cool fridge door
& gulp overripe peaches in the dark.
Remember that you've starved for three days. Lick the nectar
/ sweat / water / blood running down your forearm.
Sweet god.

☑ *Play*

tag on the playground by yourself. Watch
out—it's your shadow beside you. You feel naked
in the moon's scrutiny, except for your pool-blue hair
bobbing like a lost jellyfish on the swing. At the top
you feel weightless—you might even kill yourself
without anyone noticing, the strange upward
tug of falling beckoning you out of the Earth.
Rust-scented palms & sweat-slick hair, oh
you could set on fire at any moment.

When I die I want to become the patron saint of small fires

like matches in a blackout
a stubborn birthday candle
& the last flame at a candlelight protest.

It's not that I would like to go to heaven
but I would like to hear my name
whispered desperately in a prayer.

To become an eternal home.
Today I worship St. Teresa of Ávila,
patron saint of headaches

& St. Drogo, patron saint of ugly people.
Unfortunately, to become a saint, two miracles
must come true in your name.

Since I cannot guarantee the revival
of your dead uncle or the cure of your cancer,
I will have to bullshit my miracles poet-style.

Like, isn't it a miracle that the moon
is above the fire tonight & we are together
sharing this fleeting moment?

Isn't it all a miracle?
When you are investigating my life
to determine if I was holy enough

I hope you find
that I laughed too much
& I started too many small fires

& I compensated for my lack of grace
with my abundance of love.

Summer Elegy

Our chlorine-soaked bodies hung
        in the flammable July heat to disinfect
from all of our grimy, petty sins.

Stealing gum, burning insects,
        & falling in love with too many things.
Sleeping in laundry rooms

& soothing our thirst with the storm water.
        Sinning all over again in the crumb rubber
wrestling for the ball

or for nothing
        except for the sensation
of our squishy red torsos colliding.

For your freckles jumping
        on my tongue like popping candy.
Strawberry-blond hair wrapping around my thighs.

There was nothing to be scared of.
        We committed every sin repentable
with chlorine until our shins bruised green.

To give yourself to the grass
        & face the blueness of the sky
is to understand why your mother kneels

in front of a god. We need something to worship
        besides each other.
This is all liquid dreams. Past tense.

There's not enough space for the two of us
        anymore. Not in this small change room
where our breaths undress each other

& desire finally carves its own name
        on my tender skull.
Every poem is an elegy for a past or a future.

Summer Ode

Every August poem is a bad love poem.
        We lie down in pastel-sky graveyards

heads on gravestones, lives underneath
        us. White tails gallop across summer.

We follow their droppings into heaven.
        I hope this sainthood is not a phase.

I hope my fists are pomegranates
        & you can coax the treasures out

with your shining teeth. The words
        I wanted on our gravestones: deciduous,

buoyant, philocalist, alive. My shadow
        has outgrown me. This is a funeral

for all that we've lost to get here.
        If we grow up to be boring, love me

back into wildness.

Fucking Ohio

Columbus, Ohio. Fucking Ohio. Fuck its lumbering sky weighing down my shoulders. There's only two types of weather here: raining & almost raining. That's why the towels on your clothesline are perpetually wet. Time is forever here & still we have to grow up by tomorrow so why don't we get all this youth out of our systems. Drown in rainwater & shotgun canned kombucha & die unconventionally & write love poems. i wish dawn might never catch us. i would watch fireflies & listen to you read Siken poems forever. Being young is just a perpetual healing. New liver, same pain & all worth it for the fire. Bite my shoulder, kiss my wound, do it all over again until the dawn finds us, sprawled in the wet grass. Then we'll bleach the grass stains out of our clothes & hang our yesterdays on the clothesline & relearn perpetuity.

Manifesting Girlhood

No god, no carbs, no helmets
only falling. This is how we become girlhood.
How many summers
did we waste saturating our skies
& candying strawberries to prove
to god that we can always be sweeter?
Disappearing under our mothers'
church clothes, we dressed up as women
wanting to escape our own flesh.
Each day opened like a pop can
our wriggling limbs soft & sun scraped
kicking soccer balls with our bare feet
before we learned shame in skin.
We were unturned peaches
sweet on one side & green on the other
waiting. i bled only in my sleep
woke up to my bedsheets stained the colour
of my cheeks & said *period*
like the end of my sentence as a girl.
How many boys did i kiss
trying to lure girlhood inside me?
Lingerie & Tylenol hidden in sock drawers
jean pockets stuffed with condoms
& his breaths.
How many girls have i wanted to be
& be with.
i've learned women & desire as synonyms.

The sun bouncing off her naturally
        as if girlhood was sewn for her.
This was still when i prayed before every meal
        or was it when i stopped eating
to stop accidentally thanking god. Monster
        drinks & heat & rusted hearts
is all we ate for weeks.
        How many summers did we end
like eyelids closing reluctantly for a prayer?
        Saying it was a summer worth ending
because it would end without us anyway.
        Oh girlhood. i cut crop tops out of sunsets
made scrapbooks of bleached hair & pretty scars
        all to please you.
Please, stay a little longer.

Manifesting Boyhood

Maybe my father blamed me

for killing his hope of a son.

i've tried

to fill the son-shaped hole in his heart:

killed small things

& memorized Joseon kings

& deconstructed women.

Father was cutting

violets in our yard

when he said

No need for beautiful things.

There are bruises on my neck

in the shape of his voice.

Maybe Father blamed himself.

Blue eyes & deafening voices

guttural—all of his fantasies

of America & its sons.

i've learned boys & longing as synonyms.

i always want

what i cannot love.

My throat is stuffed

full with patrilineality.

i practise envy

but when the boy's thighs press into

mine

i search for divinity

in the cuts on his face.

i cannot blame my father

for wanting a son.

Oh beautiful boy.

Steal my hitched breath

& hide it where i cannot reach.

Teach me the consequences of the

sin of being a woman.

Mother Recites Her Will to Me

1.

When your grandmother was cremated,
the fire sounded like her screaming
or maybe laughing or maybe being freed.

The only thing gleaming through her ashes
was the metal in her back that stapled
her together clumsily like how a naive

& inexperienced god may mend a mangled
person: metal & too much love.
She pulled out all her teeth

because the dentist cost more than herself,
if she had no teeth, how could teeth
hurt her?

Her favourite flowers were daffodils.
She fell into the pond because her reflection
had teeth, she never knew she could be so beautiful.

She sewed for a living & sewed all our clothes & all our lives too.

II.

When I die, burn me.
Melt my golden tooth & make it a necklace
& throw the rest of my ashes into the ocean

alongside some daffodils. All my life
I stepped into the water expecting it to split
into the promised land, instead I drowned

every time, I loved God anyway. Her reflection
in the ocean always had a white smile. I'm sorry
for pulling out your teeth

but they grew back, didn't they? Living
is so expensive here.
Listen.

There isn't always a reason why something is beautiful.
Daffodils are beautiful,
your grandmother's gums were beautiful,

& I plan to be beautiful
as I sink to the ocean floor
& I want you to be beautiful

wearing my teeth around your neck.

How Poetry Was Invented

the day after god left me i woke up a poet.
my organs: tangles of words running between satin bones.
i think poetry was not invented but real-ized
when Eve bit that goddamn fruit & realized
that her every orifice was hollowing for more.
because i've spent the past hour reimagining you
& ended with the word *visceral*
& how could i still call myself an artist
as if my art is voluntary?
poetry is a necessary sin.
so pass over the damn fruit
& teach me *viscera.*

Yesterday I was called a slur but

this morning the sky is pale blue
& the low-hanging clouds are kissing the ground.
Two rabbits are chasing each other
leaving footprints on the fresh snow
& I hold my breath
like a rein on a wild horse
as if I could trample the beauty of this moment.
Maybe I am supposed to remember
a cold & distant winter, a memory
from my home however many miles away.
Maybe in another poem, I find the rabbits
in red pieces, taking their last breaths
on the snow
& I think of war, grieve girlhood.
But not now. In this poem
the rabbits are still alive
& wherever I go, I am home.
I have enough language
to call the rabbits angelic.
The snow crunches under their feet
& I let go of my breath.
I have enough strength to grieve.

정 情 jung

Love Poem Between Countries

All migration comes from a need.

In this train i am migrating

to Busan in need

of her, down the same road

my grandmother rushed through

during the War.

i learned about species movement

in biology picking apart a pig's heart.

Did you know that once a pig heart

beat inside a human?

During the War my grandmother ravaged

pig guts & fish scales

& last breaths & girls.

i've forgotten my grandmother's name.

But i remember

the time my mother said

homosexuality is a rich person's disease:

girls wouldn't like girls

if they were hungry.

The train is flowing

past roads built on bones

too fast to remember every death.

It's okay.

i'm not the future they died for.

The girl licks all the open sores of history

out of my mouth

& i lick all the fresh cuts out of hers.

Are we transferring wounds?

i love her

to love what i could have been.

Girl whom the salt water

recognizes by taste.

Girl who knows her grandmother's name.

We dip our feet in our shared ocean.

She reads me her favourite quotes from

South of the Border, West of the Sun:

I'm not blaming you for falling in love

with another woman.

She asks me to read to her in English

where anything sounds beautiful.

But i cut my tongue on a broken country

& my English tastes like blood.

i stare at the shadows of fish

swimming past our feet

& think about eating one alive.

i am trying to be hungry

but i keep hungering

for all the wrong things.

i start falling in love

with borderless oceans & every last breath.

We promise to be better mothers

than all of our mothers.

We promise to remember

every sacrifice however fast

they become dust behind us.

We promise to not eat all the beautiful things.

How to LOSE 10 Lbs in 5 DAYS

1. Hate Yourself

If the body can count
it is accountable for its own mistakes.
The best exercise is standing naked
in front of a mirror for 10 minutes.
The mirror is an open doorway to a horror movie.
This frame, a doorway to every past.

2. Don't Eat

Since sixth grade I have prayed
for an eating disorder.
If I could go back in time
I want to tell the girl *The softness of your skin*
is more than a sacrifice
but instead I tell her to pray harder.
In the green of summer, I stopped eating
in a victory dance. Learned the virtue
of nonpossession. The process of becoming god.

3. Exercise 2 Hours Every Day

Every step hits the ground
like a fall
as if gravity is a punishment.
The heart is tiring itself.
How much longer do we last?

4. Only Drink Tomato Juice

The boy grazes my thighs as if weighing
an animal to butcher. How much will be made
into meat, into mouth. Green foods:
granola / cigarettes / apple cider vinegar /
pictures of Pinterest girls /

5. Hate Yourself

My tween jeans are stuck in the closet.
Mother says I was so pretty
in the sixth grade.
The carcass is a block of darkness. Celebrate
the one-year anniversary of missing
my period with a new pair
of Old Navy's 12-year-old girl's leggings.
Have you lost yet?

lotus flower blooming into breasts

   i watch with hollow eyes. Relinquish everything
i once knew to let the languid motions of the film enter me
   roughly. The woman *kissing*

something probably. Her: a beautifully vacant orifice
   but for now, overflowing with something like hunger
that i swallow greedily. Her: red drool cutting through my lips.

My father changes the channel to a documentary
   about the War to teach me how to properly love in Korean:
roped naked women bruised beautiful on military trucks.

Love: soldiers slicing open white dresses
   in search of a blood mine to satiate their thirst.
Love: a revenge for existence.

The little boy is a wannabe soldier
   determined to conquer this body. i wear this skin
& call it his. Inside me his fingers become spears

puncturing dead meat & i hope to flood
   the battlegrounds with rivers of leaking red. Flickers
of his cigarette land suicide missions on my skin.

i watch with hollow eyes. Relinquish myself
   into another present: a pond overflowing with hunger.
White lotus flowers blooming into soft breasts & i

pluck its petals lovingly.
He loves me not, she loves me not
he loves me not, she

plants misty kisses on my collarbones. i
dig them up softly
before they are tainted with me: your tenderness

has no place on this body
littered with cigarette burns blooming
into bullet wounds, stars across the rib cage. Dear Father

i wish i could teach you love.
Change the channel to her lips again: a hole swallowing its orifice
& breathe light into the dusk of your eyes.

Father, this is my first lesson: there are flowers that bloom in water
& boys with quivering hands
& women who love women

& daughters
who learn how to
love.

unreliable narrator & her unreliable love stories

After-hours of a stranger's party.
Dancing in your tiny bathroom & slipping on the teal tiles to bruise
another elbow. You whispered that when you grew up you wanted to become
something neither of us could imagine
& i kissed you.
You were throbbing at the seams with uncontained hope.
You looked like you were either going to explode a city
or shrink
into a button
& what is more lovable than impossible promises.

We blew out the sun like a candle
of an unwanted birthday. Passed a man on the side of a country road
elegizing roadkill or burying lives.
Either timeline i fell in love
& cracked my forehead on the side mirror
& imaginations started spilling from the cut.
You started driving faster than we could afford
as if you wanted to crash
into the night
to see if anybody might bury us.

Seaside town & all of its dizzy scents
& sick heat. i forgot the weight of my own spine in the water
& thought i could hold you forever.
The mosquitos ate away our husks
but the sky was just blueing
& we were drenched in the romance of the beginning of melancholy
so i said *This is a small price to pay for another life.*
It is so easy to be a martyr if you believe
martyrdom will save you from dying.
God, is it morning already?
i am trying to speak in metaphors because i am scared.
i need you to read between the lines
of my ribs. My heart itching with mosquito bites.

We've lived thousands of lives
on this bathroom floor. This hair-covered, vomit-covered,
vodka-covered, lipstick-covered,
hair-dye-covered floor.
This was when the emptiness was returning to us in stranger-parties
& realism & mosquito bites that renew themselves every night.
We ignored this by kissing closed the bulky space between us.
You asked *Why do we bury people?*
Does something grow out of us?

i fantasized about the man on the highway
but i didn't fall in love this time. *i wish an ocean grows out of me.*
Or a tomato bush.
i stopped imagining you
so you could become anything when you grew up.

Parasocial Romance with Language

i fell in love with Language
        when she said *i'll never let you go*
& i thought she was speaking to me.

i've fallen in love with something
        that kisses too many lips.
Can i get jealous when i see her

dancing with someone else & she sways
        like she never has before?
i've done everything to keep Language

mine. Wrote her love poems
        & studied flash cards & held her
name in my mouth like a bird ready to fly.

Alone at night i imagine her
        skin on mine, mourning
her eventual leaving.

i watch her leave the bed in the morning.
        The birds have taken flight.

Mosquitos

I mowed the lawn this morning
sweat pooling behind my hair

sticking doggedly to my neck like cicadas
to life. Drank lemonade & showered cold.

The dog returned from the yard
green feet & smelling like young grass

like wind, like bird chirps, like fresh breaths.
I put my cheeks to his fur

& heard the Earth rustling.
Dear, I have finally found a home

worth returning to. Come in.
Sorry about the mosquitos.

Did you know that one mosquito
can return to the same person for more?

How does it feel to be a home
worth returning to?

Manic Pixie Dreams

Blue hair & ocean laughter
following seconds behind us.
Here is the setting: us
on your motorcycle
flashing neon in the night.

Fast enough the past can't catch up to us.
Behind you my fingers curl
around your pulsing ribs
& i bury my nose
in the crook of your neck
lick the shivers off your wind-rusted jaw.

i want more of you
until there is nothing left.

Exhibit A:
When we drive past red-brick yellow-door houses
that we'll never have
i still imagine you
painting the window panels & me
watering the flowers.
Not that i want this.

We were each other's manic pixie dream girls.
i wanted you
to be my practice run.

i sharpen my teeth on your Adam's apple
& map your spine on ephemera.

Do you see why i needed you to be more?
You speed up until the houses blur
into the landscape.
You told me you wanted to kill yourself
& i asked how.
How am i losing what i never had?
Our hunger for each other is the type to leave
you emptier.
Time: coming
coming
coming.
Is it all ending?
Say yes.
Say no.
Say it with your own sweet mouth
& tell me it's okay to want you.
i would drown for you.
i would drown you if you asked.
i am offering you
something more pragmatic than love.

Take it or leave it.

Love Confession for My Mother

dear Mother, your name is flowering inside mine.
let's sit & fold mandu seven years ago & laugh
& forget about all the moons in the sky.

i met the girl behind Grandma's grave.
we devoured each other, hungry not for each other
but for something incapable of staying.

dear Mother, your flour-covered fingers threaded in mine
you said you loved me the way God loves all his children:
unconditionally & with a few conditions.

i cracked my teeth on hers trying to fit
between her tongue & her words: a wet sort of heaven
her: an imperfect sort of god.

dear Mother, you taught me how to fold myself for the dead
how to bless the wilding graves with soju
how to sculpt mandu, eight pinches each, into a crescent moon

that flickered the night we stole a bottle of soju
got drunk on blessings meant for the dead &
my existence became sacrilege.

dear Mother, when i asked if God allowed us to pray
to our ancestors you said he would understand.
God is not a jerk, after all.

will God understand that my lips were
almost-prayer before being swallowed by hers?
will i go to almost-hell?

dear Mother, you said that i resemble your mother
how we both dye our nails with bongseonhwa
& believe in love & make such ugly mandu.

when will i resemble you, Mom?
we both peel our nails & love with the eyes
& make mandu with eight pinches each.

Outside this room, sweet onions are cooking

& two girls are learning
        a new song on the guitar.

The house shakes with laughter.
        I love the people in this home

these terrible, foolish people
        who have made so many mistakes

who will make so many mistakes.
        To love someone is to make a bet

that you will hold their broken hearts
        even when they don't deserve it.

Even when they cook awful eggs with onions.
        Finally, I love more than I love being loved.

Treasures I Find While Cleaning My Childhood Bedroom

how could i forget youhow could i forget youhow could i forget youhow could i forget youhow could i forget youhow could i forget youhow could i forget youhow could i forget youhow could i forget youhow could i forget youhow could i forget youhow could i forget youhow could i forget youhow could i forget youhow could i forget youhow could i forget youhow could i forget youhow could i forget you

Longing
As always, it starts with the vacuum
& soon I rummage the past & miss
my middle-school self, all the sickly skinniness
& crying. I should have died
when I was fourteen & flammable.
Then, it would have been a proper tragedy.
Since, I've wasted my summers
painting my lips red & avoiding scales
& recklessly believing in love.

Knock-Off Juicy Tubes Lip Gloss
Put it on & pretend to be stiff & sweet again,
waiting for a boy to consume me. A birthday
gift from E. Though the real gift was kissing E
(to test the lip gloss). The real gift
was that warm & orange evening
the glitter on E's front tooth.

Single Packet of Grape-Scented Condom
N shows me how to put a condom on
with my teeth & I zone out staring at her,
her closed eyes, the mechanical tenderness
in this necessity. I want to hold her
until she cries. Instead, I practise
on a toothbrush until
I am numb.

Abandoned Girlhood
I haven't spoken to E or K or N or M
for years & still, my ears are pierced & I
wear lip gloss & listen to TV Girl & pick
grape over any other flavour.

Dead Blue Lighter
that I took from the kitchen after K convinced me
she could pierce my ears with safety pins & fire.
Plug a stolen silver stud through the cut
& die laughing making DIY saline solutions.
The moon is full & pretty that night
or at least I hope it was.
Anything can be beautiful in retrospect
even the burning
& fluid-stained pillows.

Sticky Note with M's Favourite Songs
the ones M and I listened to on the school lawn,
turning golden under the June sun.
When I found out M killed herself
it had already been long since we spoke.
I didn't cry but I listened to only one song
that week. I plug in one earbud
& the other dangles in the air.

What I'm trying to say is I, too,
would like to take up space in
your tragedies.

I want to grow up

& become an almost beautiful thing.
What a blessing it is to wake up
& be beautiful
& still have room to become
more beautiful.

coming out as atheist

> "I get really offended when people tell me I'm going to hell for being bi because I feel like they're overlooking all the perfectly valid reasons I'm going to hell." —Brendon Urie

Because this is all i remember:
the pastor beating unasked-for forgiveness into my throat,
locked bathrooms & dusk-stained knees.

Because my tongue, on the way to becoming prayer,
found tenderness on hers. Because it taught me
love does not have to start on my knees pleading.

God loves all his children, even the whores & gays
even you
can be fixed.

We found warmth in each other
outside the night-filled chapel
how our lips combined into a worship for love.

Because i still feel the holy water
tracing my spine
like a snake searching for frail ankles.

We were lingering touches
smoke rings resembling trembling halos
dissolving into the hungry air.

My heart beat so close to hers
as if i was moulded from her ribs. i could
feel her whispers beating into my lungs.

When i say *forgive*
it echoes like dead prayers.
Weightless.

Because heaven must be lonely.

Because i asked for forgiveness, not repair.

Because we are young & singing
& our love is heavy enough to collapse heaven.

Why I Have Decided to Live

Spoonfuls of moonlight. Cold air. Her knit blanket

tugging at my arms to stay.

The fog resting on my shoulders, hugging me.

Summer rain through an open window.

Thunderstorms & how they change the world momentarily

unafraid, or even better, unaware of humans.

Because I left my country broken.

Because I saw the first reflection of myself in a candlelight vigil.

I was flickering.

Because we made promises.

Because I can keep trying & no one can stop me.

Peaches.

Stars.

Willow trees.

Acoustic music with a trembling voice.

The kinds of poems that give me shivers.

Trains to nowhere in particular.

Our sweat-sweet bodies colliding on wet grass.

Her hands & the way they cradle my heart

as if holding something precious.

August night drives.

Singing along to "Riptide" & eating cherries out of buckets.

Because we promised to return.

To mend a broken thing.

How laughter colonizes the lungs.

To think of myself as something larger than myself.

Because I can love every small thing.

ACKNOWLEDGMENTS

Thank you to the following publications, where versions of these poems first appeared, sometimes in different forms and under different titles: CBC Books, *Narrative Magazine, Nimrod International, This Magazine, Under the Madness Magazine,* and *Touchstone Literary Magazine.*

A special thank you to the Writers' Trust of Canada, who published some of these poems as a short collection called *diasporic dissonance* as part of the RBC Bronwen Wallace Award. Thank you for dedicating spaces for emerging writers. Thank you for believing.

A bouquet of flowers to everyone at Arsenal Pulp Press for making my dream come true, and to my editor, Natalie Wee, for beautifully expanding and evolving this book. A choir of thanks to Jazmin Welch for the cover and for your unending patience.

A bowl of hot soup to Poetry in Voice and the FutureVersers. Special acknowledgments to Thomas for inspiring the poem "can you be a poet & be happy?" and Eunsae for teaching me how to carry the boats.

Thank you to my parents for everything.

Thank you, Atlas, for being the reason I started writing this book again.

Thank you to my eighth-grade English teacher, Ms. H, for changing my life. Thank you, Ms. Araujo, for reminding me that writing is valuable and exciting.

Thanks to the normalest people I met in Ohio (and apologies to their moms) for miraculously making Columbus wild and wonderful. A plate of warm, small pretzels for Lilirose for breaking my Siken virginity and for being the best email writer.

Thanks to Hank & John Green, whom I've never met, for being my role models as writers, philanthropists, and humans.

To the people who might stop loving me after reading this book: thank you anyway. Your love until now has meant everything to me!

Here is my heart, to everyone who has believed in my work. Thank you, reader, for giving these words your own meaning.

NOTES

"Great & Green": "Tomorrow we will run faster / stretch out our arms" and "we beat on, / boats against the current / borne back ceaselessly into the past" are from *The Great Gatsby* by F. Scott Fitzgerald.

"Turing Test to Differentiate Poet & AI" is after Fiona Lu's "Turing Test."

"I hope the world ends": "both a bang & a whimper" is a reference to T.S. Eliot's "The Hollow Men."

"Last Words as Vows": "People and senators, be not affrighted" is Brutus's first spoken line after the death of Julius Caesar in *The Tragedy of Julius Caesar* by William Shakespeare.

"Mirrored Self-Portrait as Frog & Man": "what ugly rituals does it take ... & how do i perform?" is taken from Jackson Neal's "Zuko's Ode" and altered.

"Dreaming of Imaginary Wars": "A dream in which you're falling forever" is from Charles Simic's "Concerning My Neighbors, the Hittites" and altered.

"푸르다": The Korean lines are lyrics from the children's song 반달, written and composed by 윤극영 (Yoon Geuk Young).

"How to Have a Hot Girl Summer": "the strange upward / tug of falling" is taken from Savannah Brown's "Sudden fall long stop" and altered.

"How to LOSE 10 Lbs in 5 DAYS": "stopped eating / in a victory dance" is from Angel Zhao's "CBT."

"Outside this room, sweet onions are cooking": "I love more than I love being loved" is taken from Marge Piercy's "For the young who want to" and altered. Thank you, Marge Piercy, for the poem, and thank you, Sarah Tsiang, for introducing me to it.

"Why I Have Decided to Live" is after Ocean Vuong's "Reasons for Staying."

Kyo Lee is a Korean Canadian student and writer living in Waterloo, Ontario. She is the youngest winner of the CBC Poetry Prize and the youngest finalist for the RBC Bronwen Wallace Award. She loves colourful skies, summer peaches, and oceans. You can visit her online at ***kyolee.me***.